MW01295900

THE
LIES
THAT
BIND

AND THE **TRUTH** THAT SETS YOU **FREE**

STUDY GUIDE

Dr. Deborah Waterbury

ISBN-13: 9781077276314
ISBN-10: 1077276314
BISAC: Religion / Christian Life / Personal Growth

Library of Congress Control Number: 2017906017

Printed in the United States of America

The names of the people and places depicted in this book have been changed
to protect the innocent.

Scripture quotations are from the Holy Bible, English Standard Version 2000 by Crossway Books
unless otherwise noted.

INTRODUCTION

I wish that writing a book and study guide like this one wasn't necessary. However, as was evidenced in my own life and in the lives of the thousands of women I've talked to in the past few years, it wasn't only necessary, it was vital. You see, there is a battle going on every single day that many of us don't realize. That battle is for your identity.

Please don't misunderstand, though. Your identity, as the bride of Jesus Christ, is set. It's the conception of your identity that is at the center of this battle. Satan, doesn't want you to know who you are or to whom you belong. He has a myriad of reasons for this, but the main one is to keep you trapped in a mistaken identity that will not only take any possibility of joy away from you but will also render you almost completely immobile in precious Kingdom-building work.

Enter this study.

After writing *The Lies that Bind: And the Truth that Sets You Free*, I heard from hundreds, if not thousands of people who said that exposing these lies about their identity gave them a freedom they had never known. However, I also heard a lot of people tell me that reading the book, though freeing, also left them reeling from the experience of the exposure. The knowledge of the lies freed them, but it became obvious that they also needed a guide to help them in this most extraordinary and important journey.

Consequently, this study guide is just that—it's a guide. It is designed to be done in conjunction with the book and/or the video series, both of which are available at www.debwaterbury.com. The nature of the study is to dive deeper into the realities of these five lies, how you may or may not have fallen prey to them, and then replacing them with vital truths of who you actually are. The study can be done individually or in a small group, and it is best done with all three components—the book, the videos, and the study guide.

Knowing our actual identity and not the one we have been led to believe is of the utmost importance for every single believer on the planet. Each of us has a unique and wonderful role in building the Kingdom of Christ on this earth. But that role is nigh impossible when we stumble around in this life in mistaken identities. It's time that we break that cycle and rid ourselves of the chains of incorrect identities. We are the chosen bride of Christ, a royal priesthood, and a holy nation unto God. Inasmuch as this is true, it is our job to represent the beauty of what is possible only in Christ to a world that will perish without Him.

Satan hates that. He doesn't want that to happen, so he hamstrings God's most effective weapons in these false identity schemes. But we say, No more! Move toward the truth of who you are and live in the victory that is only ours in our Savior and Lord, Jesus Christ.

Your journey starts now.

CHAPTER ONE

LIE #1

"You Are Worthless"

In this insidious scheme of the enemy to derail our identities, the number one lie he uses is the lie of worthlessness, and I would venture to say that he uses this one universally. Every single one of us, at some point in our lives, began to believe that lie that we don't matter, that we aren't loved, that we are inconsequential. In short, we began to believe that we are worthless.

I realize that many people may want to contest that statement based on the fact that they never really thought those words. However, thinking the words, "You are worthless" or "You don't matter," doesn't preclude a life that bases itself on that very premise. We need only look at the choices we make to see that many of those choices have their origin in this lie.

However, and this is a big "however," the only way to vanquish the power of any lie is to expose it. And in order to expose it, you have to identify it. In other words, you have to see where you began to believe it and then name the truth instead. Are you ready to do that? Take it from me, it's not easy. As a matter of fact, you may want to do what some people do at this juncture and simply go to the next chapter or even put this book down altogether. I pray that you don't. Be brave, my friend. I promise you that the only thing waiting for you at the end of this journey is freedom.

The LIE

Satan was a murderer from the beginning, and has nothing to do with the truth, because there is no truth in him. When he lies, he speaks out of his own character, for he is a liar and the father of lies. (John 8:44, ESV)

1. Why do you think the lie of worthlessness is most likely believed by everyone at some point in their lives?

_____

_____

_____

_____

_____

_____

2. Do you agree that Satan will likely introduce this lie when we are young? Why or why not?

_____

_____

_____

_____

_____

_____

_____

3. Name some situations that might make a person begin to believe that she is worthless?

_____

_____

_____

_____

_____

_____

_____

_____

4. What kinds of choices might a person make in her life because she believes that she is worthless?

_____

_____

_____

_____

_____

_____

_____

_____

The LIE

5. Now comes the hard part: Can you think of a time when you possibly began to believe that you were worthless or that you didn't matter or that you were invisible? If you can, describe it and how it made you feel.

_____

_____

_____

_____

_____

_____

_____

_____

_____

6. What kinds of choices did you make based on that belief about your worth that you don't think you would have made had you not believed it?

_____

_____

_____

_____

_____

_____

_____

7. Why is this lie so effective in derailing believers?
   What is Satan's goal here?

   _____

   _____

   _____

   _____

   _____

   _____

   _____

Personal Thoughts:

_____

_____

_____

_____

_____

_____

_____

_____

_____

_____

_____

_____

_____

The TRUTH

Five sparrows are sold for just two pennies, but God doesn't forget one of them. Even the hairs on your head are counted. So don't be afraid! You are worth much more than many sparrows! (Luke 12:6-7, CEV)

1. In your own words, describe what Jesus did to save you?

_____

_____

_____

_____

_____

_____

2. Why do you think He did this? (Read Isaiah 53:1-12; Philippians 2:6-8; and 1 John 4:9-10)

_____

_____

_____

_____

_____

_____

_____

_____

3. The Bible repeatedly calls Jesus our "Bridegroom" and we, His "Bride." Since the Song of Solomon is a book about the love between a bridegroom and his bride, the symbolism is somewhat clear. Read the Song of Solomon 1:15; 2: 4, 6; 4:1, 7, 9. Now read Romans 8:31-39. How does your Bridegroom love you?

_____

_____

_____

_____

_____

_____

_____

_____

_____

_____

_____

_____

_____

_____

_____

_____

_____

_____

_____

_____

The TRUTH

4. Read Titus 3:4-6. How do these verses dispel any notion that the things of this life determine the level of God's love for us?

_____

_____

_____

_____

_____

_____

_____

_____

_____

_____

_____

_____

Personal Thoughts:

Our LIVES

*I have loved you with an everlasting love;
therefore, I have continued my faithfulness
to you. (Jeremiah 31:3, ESV)*

1. Read Zephaniah 3:17. What does this verse say to you about the love
   and faithfulness of God?

   _____

   _____

   _____

   _____

   _____

   _____

2. In your own words, try to summarize how God really feels about you?
   (If this is difficult, read Psalm 139:1-16.)

   _____

   _____

   _____

   _____

   _____

   _____

   _____

3. Spend some time today thanking God for His love. Praise Him, even in the midst of unbelief, and try to do it somewhere you can speak out loud. Let Satan hear you. This is powerful stuff, and your words about what is true will surely confound any plans the enemy has to lie to you any further. Now write out your own personal prayer thanking God for His unending, grace-filled, free gift of love.

CHAPTER TWO

LIE #2
"Image is Everything"

In a world where image is everything, it is no wonder that Satan loves this particular lie. And it is no wonder that it follows so closely on the heels of the worthlessness lie, since none of us wants to feel that. The issue is that just like the lie of worthlessness, this one generally takes root when we are young because we aren't even aware that we move toward image until that move has already taken place. Most often we simply stumble on this lie as we try to get out from under the awful feeling that we don't matter. Those of us who let the lie of image become one of our identity-builders do so in a vain attempt at finding worth. Unfortunately, the world tells us we have stumbled on a truth when in actuality, we've fallen in a trap that is really a lie.

Whether we want to admit it or not, pretty much all of us have bitten this bait at some point in our lives. We find the place or circumstance or look that suddenly thrusts us from outcast to insider, and one blink later, we've joined the throng of other Christians who are spinning a plethora of plates. We've joined the circus, and for a while, we like the arena. For a while. Eventually, however, there is a chasm of emptiness that becomes your life, and you can't even remember where it started.

In His love, our Father won't leave is there, though. He will deliver us from the circus, but that often requires a lot of pain as we stumble around in shards of broken glass when all of the plates fall. Where are you in this process? Are you still spinning frenetically? Have you dropped them and are now picking your way through the glass around you? Aren't you ready to stop the spin and step into peace? Then let's do it! Expose this lie and rest in the Image that has always been yours from the beginning.

The LIE

Now the serpent was more crafty than any other beast of the field that the LORD God had made.
(Genesis 3:1. ESV)

1. How do you see the world promoting this lie that "Image is Everything"?

    _____

    _____

    _____

    _____

    _____

    _____

2. How can you see this affecting our youth? How about women? (Give some examples.)

    _____

    _____

    _____

    _____

    _____

    _____

    _____

3. Why do you think having multiple images is so destructive
   to our identities?

   _____

   _____

   _____

   _____

   _____

   _____

   _____

4. Wearing multiple "hats" as a woman is different than juggling multiple
   "images." If you can, describe how you see these as two different
   things. (Hint: "Hats" are more natural than "Images" and are related to
   roles and responsibilities.)?

   _____

   _____

   _____

   _____

   _____

   _____

   _____

   _____

The LIE

5. Do you remember a time when you juggled different images according to who you were with? If so, what were they?

_____

_____

_____

_____

_____

_____

_____

_____

_____

_____

_____

_____

_____

_____

_____

_____

_____

_____

6. In all honesty, do you still spin a lot of image plates?
If so, what are they? If not, describe the instance when you stopped.

_____

_____

_____

_____

_____

_____

_____

_____

_____

_____

_____

_____

Personal Thoughts:

_____

_____

_____

_____

_____

_____

The TRUTH

*For those whom he foreknew he also predestined
to be conformed to the image of his Son, in order
that he might be the firstborn among many brothers.*
(Romans 8:29, ESV)

1. Read 1 Peter 2:1-10. What does Peter say about your identity? What does the phrase "royal priesthood" mean to you in terms of who you are?

   _____

   _____

   _____

   _____

   _____

2. What does it mean to be an "image bearer" of God? (Read Genesis 1:26-27.) Why do you think Satan wants us to believe the lie that we have to build another image to be loved?

   _____

   _____

   _____

   _____

   _____

   _____

   _____

3. Read 2 Corinthians 4:16-18 and then 3:18. What do these passages say about Christ's image and then subsequently, our image? What is important about the phrase, "are being transformed," in 3:18?

_____

_____

_____

_____

_____

_____

_____

4. Read John 17:20-26. What does Jesus' prayer say about our images?

_____

_____

_____

_____

_____

_____

_____

_____

_____

_____

Our LIVES

*God planned for us to do good things and
to live as he always wanted us to live.
That's why he sent Christ to make us what
we are. (Ephesians 2:10, CEV)*

1. What should characterize the life of someone who understands that she bears the image of Christ to a dying world?

   _____

   _____

   _____

   _____

   _____

   _____

2. How is joy closely tied to this knowledge?

   _____

   _____

   _____

   _____

   _____

   _____

   _____

3. How is all of this tied to evangelism and our ability to carry out the Great Commission? Why then do you think Satan wants to derail us here?

_____

_____

_____

_____

_____

_____

_____

_____

4. Write out some ways that you can practically live as a "royal priest" who is set apart from Satan and to Jesus?

_____

_____

_____

_____

_____

_____

_____

_____

_____

_____

CHAPTER THREE

LIE #3

"Be Strong"

Strength is a tough one. After all, everyone strives to be strong, whether that be a physical strength, an emotional strength, or a spiritual one. The world loves a strong person, and we have transported that love into our Christian walks. But that's the problem, isn't it? It's the world that has convinced us that strength is so grand; consequently, it's often the world's idea of strength that we adopt as our own.

Handle your life. Don't bother others with your problems. Keep your complaining to yourself. Don't show weakness, or someone will take advantage of you. Be all that you can be, and so on and so on. In our trek toward acceptance and love, we inadvertently slide into an ideology that being an island unto ourselves in the most desirable characteristic on earth. Where does that come from? Why is strength the mantra sung by people everywhere?

The simple answer is once again tied to the first two lies—the feeling of worthlessness and the idea that image will solve the problem—and because we are human beings with active human natures, we will naturally look to self for the answer. We look to strength in self, and that's where we go wrong. It's the origin of this elusive strength that evades us, and we end up miserable and bitter and lonely behind the barricades we build for ourselves behind that strength.

This one is slippery because it is so hard to identify. It's also difficult to manage because we so often simply don't see it. However, just like the others, once we expose the lie, it loses all power. It becomes the roach that scurries away under the light of day. So, let's shine God's flashlight on this fat, ugly roach right now. Let's call it out and call forth freedom that is only found in the strength of our Strong Tower, Jesus Christ.

23

The LIE

Put on the whole armor of God, that you may be able to stand against the schemes of the devil. For we do not wrestle against flesh and blood, but against the rulers, against the authorities, against the cosmic powers over this present darkness. (Ephesians 6:11-12, ESV)

1. How have you seen society laud strength, especially in women, throughout the ages?

_____

_____

_____

_____

_____

_____

2. Is being strong always bad? If not, name some instances when being strong in character is a good thing? When and why does this type of strength go bad?

_____

_____

_____

_____

_____

_____

_____

3. Describe some ways in which you think that Satan has used our idea of strength as a tool against Christianity.

_____

_____

_____

_____

_____

4. Name some ways that the misconception of "self-strength" led you astray.

_____

_____

_____

_____

_____

_____

5. Why does bitterness often follow the idea that we have to be strong?

_____

_____

_____

_____

_____

_____

The TRUTH

Finally, be strong in the Lord and in the strength of his might. (Ephesians 6:10, ESV)

1. Read 1 Samuel 13:1-15. How did Saul display strength in himself? What was the result?

   _____

   _____

   _____

   _____

   _____

   _____

2. Read 1 Samuel 17:31-54. How did David display strength in God? What was the result? How did this demonstrate that David was a "man after his (God's) own heart"? (1 Samuel 13:14)

   _____

   _____

   _____

   _____

   _____

   _____

   _____

3. Read Psalm 84:1-7, Philippians 4:6-7, and Hebrews 13:5-6. According to these passages, what do the people do who find their strength in God?

_____

_____

_____

_____

_____

_____

_____

_____

4. Read Ephesians 6:10-20. How does each piece of our spiritual armor depend on God for strength?

_____

_____

_____

_____

_____

_____

_____

_____

_____

_____

Our LIVES

But they who wait for the LORD shall renew their strength; they shall mount up with wings like eagles; they shall run and not be weary; they shall walk and not faint. (Isaiah 40:31, ESV)

1. What place in your life right now do you need to totally submit yourself to God's strength instead of your own? How can you do that?

_____

_____

_____

_____

_____

_____

_____

2. What characterizes a person who leans on God for strength and refuge? How do these characteristics differ from someone who is finding strength only in self?

_____

_____

_____

_____

_____

_____

_____

_____

3. How can you demonstrate "hiding behind God's shield" in a difficult situation?

_____

_____

_____

_____

_____

_____

_____

4. In your own words, describe the difference between God's shield of protection and humanity's wall of self-strength. Behind which do you find yourself right now?

_____

_____

_____

_____

_____

_____

_____

_____

_____

_____

_____

CHAPTER FOUR

LIE #4
"You Deserve This"

One of Satan's favorite strategies with binding the believer, especially as it pertains to identity, is by presenting us with half-truths. And one of his favorite half-truths is the one that speaks of what we deserve. You see, the truth from Scripture tells us that we deserve death for our transgressions. That is truth. However, and this is the part Satan likes to leave out, believers don't get what they deserve because Jesus took that punishment on our behalf. Of course, the enemy will leave that glorious part out of what he confronts us with because we will pick up the gauntlet of self when presented with the first part of this truth and try to gain deliverance under our own strength.

In short, we will try to work ourselves out of the condemnation we feel.

The problem with that is that in so doing, we also deny the gift given to us in salvation. That doesn't mean we deny repercussions for the things we do wrong, but it does mean that we deny *condemnation* for those things. That includes condemnation that may come at the hands of others.

Have you taken up that gauntlet at any time in your life? Have you allowed the enemy to lie to you about who you are in the love of the One who saved you and make you instead behave as one who has not received that new identity? This one is very tricky, but the effects it can have on how we both see ourselves and how we behave within that vision can be devastating. Break free right now, and that is also true if you have been the one moving in condemnation. Don't let Satan lie to you with half-truths. We believe the whole truth of God's Word and all of the freedom it represents.

The LIE

The thief comes only to steal and kill and destroy. I came that they may have life and have it abundantly. (John 10:10, ESV)

1. Why is believing a "half-truth" so much easier than believing a whole lie? Why do you think this is one of Satan's favorites?

_____

_____

_____

_____

_____

_____

_____

2. Think of some ways that believing the lie that we deserve condemnation is different from believing the truth that we should feel conviction over sin? (Hint: Where does each lead?)

_____

_____

_____

_____

_____

_____

3. Why do you think so many Christians struggle on the other side of this coin, with doling out condemnation instead of grace in the face of sin?

_____

_____

_____

_____

_____

_____

4. In your own words, what do we deny when we decide that we deserve punishment for our sins and then move in a direction that ensures we take that punishment in the form of condemnation from others?

_____

_____

_____

_____

_____

_____

5. Where does the lie, "You Deserve This," lead? (Hint: Believing this lie will lead to believing what other lies?)

_____

_____

_____

_____

_____

The TRUTH

*If you belong to Jesus Christ, you won't
be punished. (Romans 8:1, CEV)*

1. Read Romans 5:1-11. From where does Paul write that we receive peace?

_____

_____

_____

_____

_____

_____

_____

2. What does it mean in this passage that we have "received
reconciliation"? How can this knowledge fight the lie of condemnation?

_____

_____

_____

_____

_____

_____

_____

3. What does Ephesians 2:4-9 say about our trying to "earn" our forgiveness?

_____

_____

_____

_____

_____

4. How are "earning forgiveness" and "earning salvation" pretty much the same thing?

_____

_____

_____

_____

_____

_____

_____

5. In light of your answer to #4, read John 3:16-18. Where does condemnation actually come from?

_____

_____

_____

_____

_____

_____

Our LIVES

Little children, let us not love in word or talk but in deed and in truth. By this we shall know that we are of the truth and reassure our heart before him; for whenever our heart condemns us, God is greater than our heart, and he knows everything. (1 John 3:18-20, ESV)

1. Describe a time in your life where you may have moved in condemnation by trying to "earn forgiveness."

_____

_____

_____

_____

_____

_____

_____

_____

_____

_____

_____

_____

_____

_____

_____

_____

_____

_____

_____

_____

2. What part did other people play in that condemnation?

_____

_____

_____

_____

_____

_____

_____

_____

_____

_____

3. Have you ever found yourself on the other side of this where you were less willing to offer grace when you felt you were transgressed against? If so, why do you think that was? How might you have responded differently today than you did then?

_____

_____

_____

_____

_____

_____

_____

_____

_____

_____

Our LIVES

4. Living under the lie of condemnation can be devastating to the Body
of Christ. How do you think this is so?

_____

_____

_____

_____

_____

_____

_____

_____

_____

_____

_____

_____

_____

_____

_____

_____

_____

_____

_____

_____

_____

_____

_____

5. Find at least three (3) verses in the bible that speak of what Jesus did on the cross on our behalf. Write those verses out in your own words and pray over them, asking God specifically to break off any lies you might believe about this beautiful gift from our Savior.

CHAPTER FIVE

LIE #5

"It's Too Late"

This lie is so very devastating. It is devastating because of its seeming finality. When someone says, "It's too late," the hearer translates the message to mean, "You're finished. Nothing else matters because the chance has passed. You're done." When we believe the lie from the enemy that we've sinned too much, and therefore, it's too late for redemption, too late for reconciliation, then the hopelessness of that end can threaten to immobilize us.

And isn't that just what Satan wants?

I mean, think about it. He doesn't want you to know that with God, there is no end. He doesn't want you to realize that no sin is too much sin to erase what Jesus did on the cross for you. Because if he can get you to believe that you're just too good of a sinner to be covered by Jesus' blood, then you will give up. There is not much sadder in this life than a wonderful advocate for the love of God stifled to silence from a lie from the enemy.

The truth is that Jesus intends to use every mistake you make. Every one of them becomes a part of your story, the story that is unique only to you. Because this story is uniquely yours, it can only be told by you, and consequently, it can also be used most effectively *by you*. Don't allow Satan to gag you into submission. It's not too late. In Jesus, it's never too late.

The LIE

And the LORD said to Satan, "The LORD rebuke you, O Satan! The LORD who has chosen Jerusalem rebuke you!" (Zechariah 3:2, ESV)

1. The fifth lie in the book, "It's Too Late," is a devastating one. Why?

_____

_____

_____

_____

_____

_____

2. What does the enemy hope a person will do in believing this particular lie? What does God actually intend?

_____

_____

_____

_____

_____

_____

_____

3. How can believing this lie also be a very self-centered act?

_____

_____

_____

_____

_____

4. What is Satan claiming about Jesus when he convinces a Christian to believe that she's committed too many sins or a sin that is just too bad?

_____

_____

_____

_____

_____

_____

_____

5. "Antithesis" means that the opposite of something is true. Explain the antithesis of the lie, "It's Too Late."

_____

_____

_____

_____

_____

The TRUTH

But there's also this, it's not too late - God's personal Message! -
"Come back to me and really mean it! Come fasting and weeping,
sorry for your sins!" Change your life, not just your clothes.
Come back to God, your God. And here's why: God is kind and
merciful. He takes a deep breath, puts up with a lot, this most patient God, extravagant
in love, always ready to cancel catastrophe. (Joel 2:12-13, The Message Bible)

1. The book reminds us to look to 1 John 1:7 for comfort from this lie.
    However, if we read on in that passage to verses 8-10, how can we find
    even more comfort?

    _____

    _____

    _____

    _____

    _____

    _____

    _____

2. Read Romans 3:21-26 and summarize this great truth in your own words.

    _____

    _____

    _____

    _____

    _____

    _____

    _____

    _____

3. Think of one person in the Bible that proves that there is no such thing as "too late" in God's economy. Describe how this person's life proves this is true.

_____

_____

_____

_____

_____

_____

_____

_____

_____

4. Read the Song of Solomon 2:4. Knowing that the banqueting house was where the celebration occurred after winning a battle and the banners declared that victory, what does this verse say to you about sin and your destiny?

_____

_____

_____

_____

_____

_____

_____

_____

Our LIVES

If then you have been raised with Christ, seek the things that are above, where Christ is, seated at the right hand of God. Set your minds on things that are above, not on things that are on earth. For you have died, and your life is hidden with Christ in God. (Colossians 3:1-3, ESV)

1. Have you ever believed the lie that it's too late for you, if even for a short time? Why do you think Satan wanted you to believe it?

2. What does believing the lie, "It's Too Late," look like in a person's life?

_____

_____

_____

_____

_____

_____

_____

_____

_____

_____

_____

3. On the converse of that, what does a person's life look like who refuses to believe this lie?

_____

_____

_____

_____

_____

_____

_____

_____

_____

_____

_____

_____

Our LIVES

4. What would you say to someone who believes that she has sinned too much or too greatly to receive the gift Jesus died to give?

_____

_____

_____

_____

_____

_____

_____

_____

_____

_____

_____

_____

_____

_____

_____

_____

_____

_____

_____

_____

_____

_____

5. Write out a prayer that refutes this lie, celebrating instead the beauty of Christ's love for us.

_____

_____

_____

_____

_____

_____

_____

_____

_____

_____

_____

_____

_____

_____

_____

_____

_____

_____

_____

_____

_____

_____

_____

_____

Now
WHAT?

If you did this study the way it was intended, you probably feel one of a couple of things right now.

You may feel exhausted, and believe me, that is to be expected. You just did the spiritual equivalent of a Roto-Rooter in a clogged pipe. Exposing these kinds of deep-seeded lies is exceptionally difficult, but it is also exceptionally freeing. It's okay if you feel a little tired at first. Like I said, that is to be expected. But don't stay there. Move in your newfound identity. Bask in its lavish freedoms and thank God that even though you didn't see it for a long time, He never stopped seeing you in it.

You might be feeling like there is something you should do now, and that is also expected—because there is! Remember, you only see now as in a mirror dimly (1 Corinthians 13:12), so you only see a hint of how amazingly you are loved. I'm convinced that we wouldn't even be able to exist in the entirety of how cherished and adored we are by our Creator. Once you begin to see the beauty of this amazing truth, you're going to want to tell someone.

And there it is. There's your story. Go tell it! God designed you to have a story so that He could shine through it as a testimony to a dying world that there is only one way to Him. That way is Jesus, and our jobs here are to tell this glorious news to everyone we can. You don't have to be a great theologian. You just have to tell your story. And believe me, once you begin to see it for yourself, you realize you have some good news that you simply have to share.

However, I would be remiss if I didn't address some of you who might have done this study but haven't taken that first step toward the Savior. You may be feeling confused or even a little indignant right now. I don't blame you. I don't blame you because this would all be very confusing to read and think about if it doesn't actually apply to you. And without Jesus, it doesn't.

That's the hard news, but there is wonderful news that can follow. All that you have read and studied about identity can be true for you. Without Jesus, the things the enemy tells you about your identity are most likely true. But with Jesus, there is a greater truth that completely trumps anything Satan may try to tell you.

We all began where you are. None of us was born saved. The bible very clearly tells us that, "All have sinned and fall short of the glory of God." (Romans 3:23) The bible also tells us that the debt we owe for our sin is death, "For the wages of sin is death." (Romans 6:23) But God's love would never leave us in our own filth. He loved us way too much for that. Instead, God sent his only Son, Jesus Christ, to pay the penalty we rightfully owe for our sin. Again, the bible tells us, "But God shows his love for us in that while we were still sinners, Christ died for us." (Romans 5:8) In other words, Jesus died so that we could live.

If you have read this study and book or watched the videos, and you feel confused and lost because you haven't taken that important first step, then I have great news for you! You can take care of that right now. The bible says, "If you confess with our mouth that Jesus is Lord and believe in your heart that God raised him from the dead, you will be saved. For with the heart one believes and is justified and with the mouth one confesses and is saved." (Romans 10:9-10) That's all it takes, just confessing what you know in your heart to be true. If you are in a group, I encourage you to seek out your group members and have them share in this with you. If not, or if you prefer to do this alone, here is a simple prayer that expresses what the bible says is necessary for salvation:

Dear God,

I believe what You say is true. I believe that Jesus is Your Son, and I believe that You sent Him down to earth to give His life in payment for my sins. I believe that He is Your Son, the Son of God, and I believe that the grave couldn't hold Him because He is Your Son. I believe that He was resurrected after three days and that He lives now in heaven with You. I accept all of these things as true, and I want Jesus to be my Savior. I accept His gift on my behalf so that I, too, can live forever with You in eternal joy and peace. Thank You for this amazing gift, and thank you, Jesus, for dying on the cross so that I could live.
From this moment forward, I am a child of God and Jesus is my Lord and my Savior. Amen.

That's it! If you prayed that prayer, then all the things you've read about and studied about in the past weeks apply to you, too! You are a new creation, a beautiful soul whose eternity is secure with the Father forever. The bible clearly tells us, "For everyone who calls on the name of the Lord will be saved." (Romans 10:13) God heard you, and now you are His! There is rejoicing in heaven with your decision, I can assure you of that!

You also start from a good place, my friend. You already know that Satan is going to try to lie to you about who you are and to whom you belong. Don't let him. Call him out. Then move in the truth of who you actually are—the cherished, adored, loved bride of Jesus Christ.

Then tell somebody. It's such good news. Who would want to keep it in?

One Woman,
One Business at a Time

ABOUT THE AUTHOR

Dr. Deb currently lives in Tucson, Arizona, with her husband of thirty-two years, Jeff, and their two dogs, Levi and Hattie. She has two adult sons, Spence and Miles, both of whom are steadily moving toward God's work in their own lives. Dr. Deb is the President and CEO of Love Everlasting Ministries, an international women's ministry dedicated to breaking barriers of isolation for women everywhere through education, study, and connection to one another in the body of Christ.

Her latest project is a school for widows and impoverished women called the Reap What You Sew Project. It is a tailoring school set to launch in Blantyre, Malawi, this year. This school will offer six months of training in the trade of tailoring, as well as two weeks of business training. At the end of the six months, each qualifying student will receive the sewing machine she has been sewing on, as well as enough cloth and other materials to begin her own tailoring business. By helping women provide for themselves and their children, Dr. Deb says that, "We will help change women, their children, their villages, and finally, their nations." For more information on how you can be involved in sponsoring this school, as well as being personally connected to one of the students, please visit loveeverlastingministries.com today.

Dr. Deb is available for conferences, book signings, and retreats. Simply contact her on her website, DebWaterbury.com, where you can email her and also see her other books, podcasts, blogs, and messages available for purchase or download.

lovetruthlive

WITH DEB WATERBURY

Teaching that the love of Christ
and the Truth of Scripture lead
to life-changing freedom

*"By this all people will
know that you are my
disciples, if you have
love for one another."*
– John 13:35

debwaterbury.com

lovetruthlive

WITH DEB WATERBURY

PAINTED WINDOW TRILOGY:

Painted Window, Threads and White Zephyr

Follow Elizabeth Percy's allegorical
journey into discovering the love
that transforms all of our lives –
the love of Jesus, our Bridegroom.

James on the Mount

A study of the book of James as it relates
to the Sermon on the Mount.

DAILY DEVOTIONAL SERIES:

Bible devotional studies, verse by verse.

- *Galatians* (3 month devotional)
- *Ephesians* (3 month devotional)
- *Philippians* (3 month devotional)

WOMEN'S MINISTRY STUDIES:

6 Pairs of Sandals
Yesterday's Footsteps and Today's
Women's Ministry

SPANISH TRANSLATIONS:

Las Mentiras Que Atan

DEB WATERBURY ALSO OFFERS:

TWO WEEKLY SHOWS
on the Deb Waterbury YouTube page, podcast on iTunes.
Real Life with Deb Waterbury (new episode every Tuesday)
Get Real with Deb Waterbury (new episode every Thursday)

Windows of the Heart
(Podcast Teachings – also available through itunes)

Visit us on Facebook, Twitter, Instagram,
LinkedIn, Pinterest and YouTube

Note:
Dr. Deb Waterbury continues to expand her resource catalogue,
so please log onto her website for the most recent additions.